Brief Notes

RETAILING

The publications in *Brief Notes* are outlines of core topics of interest to professionals involved in shopping center management. The outlines are capsule overviews of each topic. Many key points are covered, and shopping center examples are provided for further illustration. Core concepts in each area guide you on topics you may want to explore further. Each outline also contains a helpful glossary.

Brief Notes is designed to provide a helpful and informative overview of the topics covered. It is not intended to be a substitute for more extensive learning that can be achieved through attending ICSC educational programs and reading additional ICSC professional publications.

The outlines contained in *Brief Notes: Shopping Center Management:*

- Management Overview
- Finance
- Insurance and Risk Management
- The Lease and Its Language
- Leasing Strategies
- Maintenance
- Marketing
- Retailing
- Security

Brief Notes

RETAILING

International Council of Shopping Centers
New York

ABOUT THE INTERNATIONAL COUNCIL OF SHOPPING CENTERS

The International Council of Shopping Centers (ICSC) is the trade association of the shopping center industry. Serving the shopping center industry since 1957, ICSC is a not-for-profit organization with over 44,000 members in 77 countries worldwide.

ICSC members include shopping center

- owners
- developers
- managers
- marketing specialists
- leasing agents
- retailers
- researchers
- attorneys

- architects
- contractors
- consultants
- investors
- lenders and brokers
- academics
- public officials

ICSC sponsors more than 200 meetings a year and provides a wide array of services and products for shopping center professionals, including deal making events, conferences, educational programs, accreditation, awards, publications and research data.

For more information about ICSC, write or call the
International Council of Shopping Centers
1221 Avenue of the Americas
New York, NY 10020-1099
Telephone: 646-728-3800
Fax: 212-589-5555
info@icsc.org
http://www.icsc.org

This publication is designed to provide accurate and authoritative information in regard to the subject matter covered. It is sold with the understanding that the publisher is not engaged in rendering legal, accounting, or other professional services. If legal advice or other expert assistance is required, the services of a competent professional person should be sought.

—From a Declaration of Principles jointly adopted by a Committee of the American Bar Association and a Committee of Publishers.

Companies, professional groups, clubs and other organizations may qualify for special terms when ordering quantities of more than 20 of this title.

Published by
International Council of Shopping Centers
Publications Department
1221 Avenue of the Americas
New York, NY 10020-1099

ICSC Catalog No.: 242

ISBN: 1-58268-028-0

Contents

Preface

I n the past, a shopping center manager's main task may have been to enforce the requirements of the lease and to collect the rent.

Now, shopping center managers are better understood to be retail property managers. It is crucial that they understand retailing to better communicate with their tenants and to help them improve their businesses. By understanding the business of retailing, a leasing strategy can be achieved more efficiently.

The task is not as formidable as it may seem. The following pages explain those key points that will help you—the shopping center professional—understand the fundamentals of retailing: how to meet consumers' needs and the various facets of day-to-day operations. Essential information about retail math and accounting is also covered to help you analyze a store's financial performance. Words and terms and concepts are clearly defined and are listed in the glossary.

Acknowledgments

The material in this outline is based in part on a course presented at the International Council of Shopping Centers (ICSC) John T. Riordan School for Professional Development Management, Marketing and Leasing Institutes.

The International Council of Shopping Centers gratefully acknowledges the individuals mentioned below, who have contributed their expertise to this publication.

Elliot Gant
John Konarski III, Ph.D.
Horace Landry
Karen Litton, SCMD, Marketing Manager, Scottsdale Fashion
    Square
Scott Sorensen, SCMD, SCSM, President, Scott Sorensen Resources, Inc.

Core Concepts

✓ Definition of retailing
✓ Retailer types
✓ Non-stores

EFFECTIVE RETAILING

R etailing comprises all activities involved in the sale of goods and services directly to the ultimate user for personal, non-business purposes.

Retailing aims specifically to provide those goods and services that will satisfy key consumer needs such as:

- Buying specific goods and services
- Meeting social needs—to communicate, to be recognized and to be served
- Being entertained
- Enjoying security and convenience

■ Informing customers of new merchandise trends and ideas

To meet these needs, a retailer is primarily concerned with having appropriate products and services, greeting people and serving them well, attracting them with visual merchandising and providing a clean, attractive store.

Retailer Types and Classifications

Retailers can be classified in a variety of ways. Among the more common are:

■ Ownership: This involves the independent store, chain, franchise, leased department, vertical integration (a company that manufactures, wholesales and retails the product) and consumer cooperative.

■ Strategy mix: This includes the traditional full-line department store, specialty department store, discount store, mass merchandiser, specialty store, category specialist (or category killer), home improvement center, wholesale club, off-price factory outlet, catalog showroom, conventional supermarket, superstore, warehouse supermarket and convenience store. (See glossary for definitions)

■ Non-store: This relates to vending machines, direct selling (salesperson contacts the customer at home or the office), direct mail, catalog, TV home shopping and e-commerce.

■ Service Retailing: This deals with rented goods, owned goods and services such as auto rental companies, auto repair and service stations, child care centers, fitness centers, home maintenance companies and income tax preparers.

Tenant Mix

Every shopping center needs a balanced mix of merchants that will directly respond to the needs of the market in terms of price, level of service offered and merchandise sold. The mix will typically include varying percentages of the following retailers:

- Department stores/anchors
- Women's apparel
- Women's specialty (intimate apparel, maternity, accessories)
- Men's apparel
- Children's apparel
- Shoe stores
- Specialty restaurants
- Fast food
- Books, cards, gifts
- Jewelry
- Home furnishings and accessories
- Misc. specialty (eyewear, health and beauty, cellular phones, etc.)
- Services (hair salons, dry cleaners, shoe repair, etc.)
- Carts/kiosks

Core Concepts

✓ Customer appeal
✓ Stock keeping units (SKUs)
✓ Customer relationship management (CRM)

Physical Layout

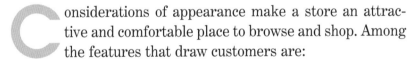

Considerations of appearance make a store an attractive and comfortable place to browse and shop. Among the features that draw customers are:

- General appearance and housekeeping
- Condition of fixtures, carpeting, windows
- Signage
- Overall store layout—width of aisles, unobstructed visibility or traffic flow, organization
- Appeal of interior color and design
- Lighting—overall, spotlight, storefront and in dressing rooms.
- Informative signage

Merchandise and Displays

As they order goods and visually present them, retailers must bear in mind the following factors:

- Selection of merchandise: This is key to meeting consumer demand for fashion and style, quality, price and seasonality.
- Depth of selection: This is an important area in terms of knowing customers and their needs. Are stock keeping units (SKUs) available in all sizes?
- Inventory: This must be adequate to sustain sales.
- Window displays: These are invaluable and should be designed to capture attention and draw shoppers. They should be changed frequently (at least as often as regular customers visit).
- Interior displays: These help sell merchandise and should feature readily visible goods well organized by category, with clearly marked prices.
- Loss prevention: Consider security issues when placing merchandise near store entrances, delivery areas and dressing rooms.

Market Perception

No store operates in a vacuum. To meet consumer need and fill a place in the market successfully, store management must be aware of:

- Consumer perception of the store: What is the store's image and service level?
- The characteristics of the store's customer: Who is the store's core customer? Who is the store's target audience?

- Store management's perception: If this differs from consumer perception, how is the store responding?
- The characteristics of the store's customer: What are the average age range, income bracket, expenditures, and so on? Also, how does the sales staff rate in terms of familiarity with or recognition of individual regular customers?
- Its market demographics: How does the store attract more customers?
- Its competition: What merchandise do they feature? What services do they offer? What do they do well or poorly? How do their prices compare?
- Convenience of hours: Are there "special hour" options for those who can't shop during the day?
- Store security: Is there a security officer on duty? Is the parking area well lit?

Advertising and Promotion

Both are designed to reach beyond the store itself to communicate the store's message to the public and draw customers. Advertising may focus attention either on products or on store image. Promotions generally are aimed at sparking specific purchases and can involve:

- Target audience
- Allocation of dollars
- Choice of medium: direct marketing (snail mail, e-mail, telephone), newspapers, magazines, radio, outdoor, yellow pages, television, Internet Web site
- Type of promotional event: special sales, enter to win opportunities, contests, gifts with purchase, fashion shows, demonstrations, customer coupons/incentives, frequent shopper programs

- Participation in center-wide advertising and sales events
- Cooperative advertising that may include tie-ins with similar stores or offer special opportunities

Management and Staffing

Salespeople and store managers alike must be well trained, well informed and service oriented to meet the needs of customers who have become better educated, more demanding and more convenience oriented. Elements in this area to consider are:

- Experience and professionalism of store management
- Adequate staffing by trained salespeople
- Management and staff knowledge of store policies and merchandise
- Record of staff turnover

Sales Skills and Customer Service

Successful salesmanship is based primarily on "people skills," but this must be backed up by merchandise knowledge. The basic criteria of sales service by which to judge a salesperson are:

- Greeting customers: Acknowledging them warmly and quickly. Step back and say "Hello"; do not confront them by approaching and saying "May I help you?" Instead ask a question that will not produce a customer response of "yes" or "no."
- Determining needs: Asking about a customer's needs and preferences through open-ended—what, where, when, why, who or how—questions. And listen, listen, listen.

- Suggesting specific merchandise that meets the customer's needs.
- Presenting the merchandise: Showing the merchandise to its best advantage and overcoming customer reservations.
- Knowing the features and benefits of the merchandise: Being aware of the materials that items are made of as well as the qualities the fabrics and construction provide; offering suggestions for use and care, giving fashion advice and suggesting additional merchandise that is related to the original item(s)
- Closing the sale: Helping the customer make a decision.
- Being familiar with store procedures: Knowing how to complete the transaction, process credit cards, obtain a quick price check if scanner fails.
- Customer Relationship Management (CRM): Having systems in place to connect with the customer on a regular basis. Having a Web site where customers can research more about the products and services as well as purchase directly on a 24/7 (24 hours, seven days a week) basis. Instituting a preferred customer loyalty program offering special incentives and communication. Having software systems to track customer transactions individually so as to better serve their needs.
- Building a future relationship: Thanking customers for shopping and inviting them to return. Keeping a record of customers' purchases and needs to better serve them in the future through sale notifications, thank-you postcards, etc.

Key Consumer Influences

Understanding what influences customers to shop—or to stop shopping at a given store—can help retailers realize where they must focus their attention, as follows:

- Reason for purchase: Of all the elements of retail operations noted above, the one that most influences a consumer decision to purchase is service. The reasons for purchase include the physical appeal of the store—its visual merchandising, music, fragrance, lighting, overall atmosphere; price and value; fashion and style; service; the sales representative's attitude, product knowledge, ability to find the product to meet the customer's needs and wants.

- Reasons for "quitting" the store: The overriding reason that people stop shopping at a given store is lack of service. People quit a store for many reasons, including (their own) death; moving away; negative word-of-mouth; ordinary competitive reasons (a store remodeled or opened closer to the customer); dissatisfaction with a purchased product; shopper-perceived indifference by a store representative; an argument with a salesclerk.

Core Concepts

✓ Sales per square foot
✓ Comparison by retail classification
✓ Occupancy costs

HOW TO EVALUATE A RETAILER'S PERFORMANCE

Sales Reports

Monthly, quarterly and annual sales reports will reflect increases or decreases in sales performance. (The section on financial statements that follows offers tools for analyzing financial performance.) It is useful to compare:

- Sales of merchants within like retail classifications
- This year's sales (in dollars and units) versus last year's
- Percentage increase in sales per category
- Sales per square foot versus the average for the category within the center, the average for the category regionally

and nationally, and the overall center sales per square foot.

- Occupancy costs as a percentage of sales

Typically a tenant's occupancy costs run from 10 to 12 percent of annual sales. These costs (sometimes referred to as tenancy costs by retailers) include rent (minimum and overage), common area maintenance (CAM), real estate taxes, insurance and marketing fund paid to the landlord. They do not include utilities, sales help, etc. Occupancy costs exceeding 12 percent usually indicate a tenant in trouble. Exceptions are food court tenants, which can pay as high as 18 percent of their sales in occupancy costs.

Store Audits

Store audits may be used to assess a store's strengths and weaknesses (see Appendix: Tenant Audit, pages 31–35). In this context, a store audit is different from an accounting audit of a store's sales to verify the tenant's sales reporting responsibilities under the lease. A store audit instead helps the landlord and tenant to receive an independent assessment of the store. Landlords usually share the results of the audit with the retailer. One approach would be to use a retail checklist to evaluate a specific aspect of every store every day. In general, it is important to consider:

- Store appearance: Windows, flooring, carpeting, lighting, signage
- Inventory: Timeliness, stock levels (depth and breadth)
- Merchandise presentation: Windows, entrances, mannequins, signs, lighting, finishes of display fixtures
- Sales staff: Appearance, salesmanship, friendliness, knowledge, customer service

- Management: Experience, attitude
- Marketing: Awareness, participation, ability to draw customers with the store's own marketing programs

Market Research

To understand the retailer's market, it is important to look for information beyond the store itself, which can include:

- Industry averages: A general knowledge of average national sales figures for a given retail category (broken down by month or season and region) will help you evaluate the performance of a store in that category.
- Competition: What is the store's competition? Has it changed recently? What does the competition do well or poorly? How has the merchant responded? When reviewing competition, it is important to look beyond the traditional competition. For instance, a drugstore's major competitors for prescription drugs might include supermarkets, wholesale clubs, mass merchant supercenters and direct mail.
- The marketplace: Is the store's market changing? Is it getting older? Are traditional nuclear families moving in or are they disappearing? Is minority and ethnic influence growing? What is the reaction to this change?
- Consumer reaction: What do they like and dislike about stores in the center? What changes or additions would they like to see?
- What market shares do the retailers have? Can they increase them? How?

Core Concepts

✓ Cost of goods minus discounts (net price)
✓ Dating
✓ DOI, ROG

DISCOUNTS

The following terms and equations are the essentials of retail math: how to calculate the wholesale prices that merchants pay to vendors; how to determine markups, markdowns and the ultimate retail price to the consumer; how to evaluate inventory stock turnover; and how to measure profits. The place to begin is with discounts that are designed to encourage the prompt payment of bills.

Trade Discounts

The trade discount is the manufacturer's or supplier's discount from the suggested list price; it is expressed as a percentage. Along with the list price—the retail price, suggested or recommended by the manufacturer—it is used to determine the net price.

■ The net price (or retailer's cost price): This is the amount a retailer must pay to the supplier for a particular piece of merchandise. To find the net price, multiply the list price by the trade discount percentage and then subtract the result from the list price.

Example: A baseball glove has a suggested list price of $50. The retailer is offered a trade discount of 40%. The net price would be $30, computed as follows:

$$\$50 \times .40 = \$20$$
$$\$50 - \$20 = \$30$$

More simply, multiply the list price by the complement of the trade discount percentage (the complement, which is the difference between 100 and the trade discount, will be used in all examples that follow):

$$\$50 \times .60 = \$30$$

Series Discounts

A series discount represents a number of discounts offered by the manufacturer to a retailer. To find the net price, multiply the list price by each discount percentage in succession.

Example: A line of towels has a suggested list price of $20 each. The retailer is offered a series of discounts of 30%, 10% and 5%. To determine the net price, multiply each percentage:

$$\$20 \times .70 = \$14$$
$$\$14 \times .90 = \$12.60$$
$$\$12.60 \times .95 = \$11.97$$

The net price is $11.97.

Cash Discounts

A cash discount is an inducement by the manufacturer or wholesaler to persuade the retailer to pay promptly. It consists of the following parts:

- A percentage discount
- A period of time in which the discount may be taken
- A net period that determines the date by which the full amount of the invoice must be paid.

Dating may be calculated from three points in time:

- Date of invoice (DOI) dating: DOI indicates that the discount period for prepayment of the invoice and the due date for the full amount of the invoice begin on the first day after the date of the invoice.

    Example: A hardware store receives an invoice for a shipment of nuts and bolts for $1,000 dated February 10, with terms of 3/10 N 30 DOI. (The first number, 3, represents the percentage of discount. The second number, 10, represents the number of days you have to take advantage of the discount. The letter N followed by a number—in this case, 30—represents the number of days in which you have to pay the entire bill. The last letters—DOI here—indicate the date from which you count the number of days.) Figure the alternate payment dates and the amounts due for this invoice if the invoice is paid within ten days to take the maximum discount as follows:

    $$\$1,000 \times .97 = \$970$$

    The discounted price is allowed on payments up to February 20, or the entire $1,000 is due on March 10.

■ Receipt of goods (ROG) dating: ROG indicates that the discount period for prepayment of the invoice and the due date for the full amount of the invoice begin on the first day after receipt of the merchandise.

Example: A sporting goods retailer receives an invoice for golf balls for $2,000 dated May 15, with terms of 2/10 N 30 ROG. The merchandise is received on May 25. The alternate payments dates to receive the maximum discount if the invoice is paid within ten days from the time the golf balls were received and the amount due for this invoice are calculated as follows:

$$\$2,000 \times .98 = \$1,960$$

This amount is payable until June 5. The entire $2,000 would be due on June 25.

■ End of month (EOM) dating: EOM indicates that the discount period for prepayment of the invoice and the due date for the full amount of the invoice begin on the first of the next month. If the invoice is dated after the twenty-fifth of the month, the discount period for the prepayment and the due date for the full amount begin on the first of the next month.

Example: A toy store receives an invoice for dolls for $3,000 dated June 5, with terms of 4/10 N 30 EOM. The alternate payment dates to receive the maximum discount and the amounts due for this invoice are calculated as follows:

$$\$3,000 \times .96 = \$2,880$$

This amount is payable until July 10. The full amount would be due on July 30.

Example: A jewelry store receives an invoice for fashion watches for $10,000 dated June 29, with terms of 2/10 N 30 EOM. Calculate the alternate payment dates to receive the maximum discount and the amounts due for this invoice as follows:

$$\$10,000 \times .98 = \$9,800$$

This amount is payable until August 10. The full amount would be due on August 30.

Core Concepts

✓ Markup formulas
✓ Keystone markup
✓ Markup is expressed as a percentage of selling price (not cost)
✓ Gross margin
✓ Net profit

MARKUP

The markup is the difference between the retail selling price of the merchandise and the cost of the merchandise. Markup can be expressed in dollars or as a percentage. As an equation, it is expressed as follows:

$$\text{Retail (R)} = \text{Markup (MU)} + \text{Cost (C)}$$
$$\text{or}$$
$$\text{Markup} = \text{Retail} - \text{Cost}$$
$$\text{or}$$
$$\text{Cost} = \text{Retail} - \text{Markup}$$

Example: A baseball glove was purchased from a manufacturer by a retailer for $30 and sold for $50. The markup was $20, figured as follows:

$$\$50 - \$30 = \$20$$

When markup is expressed as a percentage of retail, almost all retailers express it based on retail, not cost. As an equation, it is expressed:

$$\text{MU\% on Retail} = R - C/R \times 100$$

Example: If a sweater sold for $80 and cost the retailer $50, the MU% would be 37.5% as the equation shows:

$$(\$80 - \$50) \div 80 \times 100 = 37.5\%$$

Keystone markup is a very typical markup used by retailers. It is double the cost or 50% of the selling price.

Example: If a pair of gloves sold for $40 and cost the retailer $20, the MU% would be 50% or keystone as the equation shows:

$$(\$40 - \$20) \div 40 \times 100 = 50\%)$$

Initial Markup

Markup is affected by reductions like employee discount, stock shortages (known as shrinkage) and markdowns, as well as by alteration expenses and cash discounts. Initial markup takes all those factors, as well as operating expenses and net profit, into consideration; it is the first markup placed on an item, and it is used to calculate the original retail price at which the merchandise will be sold. As an equation, it is expressed:

$$\text{Initial markup (IMU)} = (\text{operating expenses} + \text{net profit} + \text{alteration expense} + \text{reductions} - \text{cash discounts}) \div \text{net sales}$$

Maintained Markup

This is the difference between the net sales and the gross cost of merchandise sold by the net sales. As an equation, it is expressed:

Maintained markup (MMU)% = IMU% (100% + reductions %) − reductions %

or

Maintained markup $ = IMU% (net sales $ + reductions $) − reductions

Example: A buyer of a department expects to have reductions of 5% during the coming season and plans an initial markup of 40%. Calculate the maintained markup planned by the buyer as follows:

$$.40 \times 105 = 42\%$$
$$.42 - .05 = 37\%$$

Markdown

To determine the markdown percent that a retailer may take to achieve a specific maintained markup if he or she has established the initial markup, the retailer uses the formula:

Reductions % = (IMU% − MMU%) ÷ (1 − IMU%)

Example: A toy department plans an MMU% of 40%. The buyer's initial markup for the department is 45%. Calculate the maximum markdown percent the buyer could take as follows:

$$(.45 - .40) \div (1 - .45) = .09 \text{ (or 9\%)}$$

Gross Margin

Gross margin (GM) is the final markup that is obtained by the retailer upon selling the merchandise in inventory. As an equation, it is expressed:

Gross Margin =
- Initial markup %
- Minus markdowns, alteration costs and shrinkage at cost (%)

Gross Margin %

Example: Initial markup 45%
 —Markdowns at cost 6.6% (12% × .55)
 —Shrinkage at cost 1.1% (2% × .55)
 —Alteration costs (none)

$$
\begin{array}{r}
37.3\% \\
+ \text{ Discounts } \quad 3.0\% \\
\hline
40.3\%
\end{array}
$$

Example of markup (initial)
 Markup . . . 60%
 Cost ÷ inverse of $^{40}/_{60}$* = selling price
 $8 ÷ .40 = $20

Selling price − cost ÷ selling price = markup
$20 − $8 = 12 ÷ 20 = .60 (60%)

*Note: The inverse of 60% is 40%, which equals to 100%. Likewise the inverse of 35% is 65%, which equals to 100%.

> # Core Concepts
>
> ✓ BOM and EOM inventory
> ✓ Stock turns

STOCK TURNOVER

Stock turnover measures the degree of balance between the retailer's inventory and the retailer's sales, and the speed with which merchandise moves into and out of a department or store. Stock turnover can be calculated in units; however, it is usually calculated in dollars. As an equation, it is expressed:

Unit stock turnover = number of units sold
÷ average stock for the period in units
or
Stock turnover at retail = net retail sales
÷ average inventory at retail in dollars
or

Stock turnover at cost = net cost sales
÷ average inventory at cost in dollars

Average Inventory

To calculate stock turnover, first determine the month's average inventory. As an equation, it is expressed:

Average inventory = BOM (beginning of the month)
+ EOM (end of month) ÷ 2

Example: If 50 stuffed animals are in stock at the beginning of the month and there are 20 stuffed animals at the end of the month, the average inventory (50 + 20 ÷ 2) is 35.

To find the average inventory for a season, add up the BOMs and divide by the number of BOMs in a season. Remember that a six-month season has seven BOMs.

Example: If the number of ⅛-inch gold chains in stock over a six-month period is 5 on January 1, 25 on Feburary 1, 20 on March 1, 15 on April 1, 30 on May 1, 25 on June 1 and 20 on July 1, the average inventory is 20.

Impact of Stock Turnover on Sales

The relationship between stock turnover and sales can be seen in the following equations:

Stock turnover = net sales ÷ average stock
or
Average stock = net sales ÷ stock turnover
or
Net sales = average stock × stock turnover

Example: A men's necktie shop has an average inventory of $300,000 at retail for a year, with a planned stock turnover of 3. Calculate the sales that are required to reach the planned turnover as follows:

$$300,000 \times 3 = 900,000$$

Example: A ski shop has planned net sales of $2,000,000, with a planned stock turnover of 3. What should the store's average stock be?

$$2,000,000 \div 3 = 666,667$$

The number of times merchandise turns over has a dramatic impact on overall profits. Just one more turn can make the difference between profitability and loss. (An additional stock turn can translate into just one extra item sold to each customer.) Compare Store A and Store B below. Notice that they have identical costs for inventory and expenses:

	Store A	Store B
Number of turns	4	3
Sales	$1,000,000	$750,000
Average inventory	250,000	250,000
Gross margins (40%)	400,000	300,000
Expenses	350,000	350,000
Profits	50,000	−50,000 (loss)

Profits

- Gross profit is markup multiplied by sales price. For example, if a shirt sells for $35 and the markup is 50%, the gross profit is $17.50.
- Net profit takes into account the cost of doing business (personnel, rent, shrinkage, markdowns, advertising and insurance costs, for instance) to calculate the actual bottom-line profit.

Core Concepts

✓ Assets equals liabilities plus net worth

✓ Sales minus cost of sales minus expenses equals net profit

✓ Ratios, acid test, working capital

FINANCIAL STATEMENTS

To assess how well a retailer is doing, it is important to read and analyze two financial statements. The balance sheet and the income statement, and the various ratios derived from them, give management the information needed to evaluate the effectiveness of past and current retail operations. Each of the financial statements and ratios provides a unique insight into the retailer's financial performance and position.

The Balance Sheet

The balance sheet shows the retailer's financial position or condition on a specific date. In simple terms, the balance sheet equation is:

$$\text{Assets} = \text{liabilities} + \text{net worth}$$

The parts of the balance sheet include:

- Assets: This is what the business owns. It consists of current assets and fixed assets. Current assets are those sufficiently liquid that they can be converted into cash within 12 months (for example, cash, accounts receivable and inventory). Fixed assets are those things that are used in the business and are not for sale (for example, real estate, leasehold improvements and equipment).
- Liabilities: Those things that can be claimed against the business; that which it owes. These include current liabilities (those due within 12 months)—notes payable (what is owed the bank or investors), accounts payable (what is owed trade vendors, suppliers), income taxes (what is owed the government)—and long-term liabilities (those owed after 12 months).
- Net worth: What the owner actually owns in the business.

The Income Statement

While the balance sheet indicates the retailer's immediate financial position, the income statement represents the retailer's financial performance over a specific period of time by showing income and expenses. The income statement shows whether investments in assets and the implementation of strategy were successful. In simple terms, the equation for the income statement is:

$$\text{Net profit (or loss)} = \text{sales} - \text{cost of sales} - \text{expenses}$$

The parts of the income statement include:

- Sales: Income during that period

- Cost of sales: The amount paid for the merchandise sold during that period
- Gross margin: The difference between the amount of sales (after returns and allowances) and the cost of the goods; the profit before the expenses
- Expenses: The charges involved with running the business, including variable expenses (also called direct expenses), those costs that can change quickly (for example, salaries based on commission); and fixed expenses (indirect expenses), those costs that remain constant (for example, rent, utilities, common fee charges).
- Net profit (or loss): The amount of money left after all expenses are paid. Literally, the bottom line.

Key Business Ratios

The following formulas are key business ratios that help analyze a business's performance with figures taken from both the balance sheet and income statement (the first four are the most commonly used). Once the equations have been calculated, the answers must be compared to industry averages to measure performance. (Such standards are available from Dun & Bradstreet and other firms.) The ratios are:

- Current assets to current liabilities: A test of liquidity—the ability to turn assets into cash—and solvency. (One assumption here is that inventory can be quickly converted into cash.)
- Quick ratio (acid test): A more rigorous test of liquidity, it eliminates certain inclusions like inventory and prepaid items like insurance. Divide quick assets (cash) by current liabilities. A result equal to at least 1 indicates the ability to pay debts.

- Net profits to net sales: A test of profitability. Divide net profits by net sales.
- Net profits to net worth: Another test of profitability, this tends to be the final one. Most accountants look for a figure of 14%. However, it is important to evaluate performance based on how long a store has been in business; a lower number might mean success for a new company but not for a more established one.
- Net profits to net working capital: A test of liquidity. Net working capital is the excess of current assets over current liabilities. The ratio is a useful indicator of day-to-day status; it looks at how much liquidity is derived from profits.
- Net sales to net worth: A measure of invested capital and how often it turns over.
- Net sales to net working capital: A test of the firm's activity; a guide to its ability to turn working capital and its level of operating funds.
- Current liabilities to net worth: A test of leverage, or the level of debt versus the level of assets. Trouble is indicated when the ratio exceeds 80%.
- Total liabilities to net worth: A test of leverage. When the ratio exceeds 100%, creditors have greater equity in the firm than the owners do (often the situation in a hostile leveraged buyout).
- Inventory to net working capital: A test of inventory balance and true capital liquidity. A ratio greater than 80% implies that day-to-day working capital is insufficient.

Core Concepts

✓ Retail sale for personal nonbusiness purposes

✓ Retailer performance

✓ Understand financial statements

CONCLUSION

Retailing combines all those activities involved in the sale of goods and services to the user for personal, nonbusiness purposes. Retailers come in many styles (department stores, specialty stores, mass merchandisers, to name but three), and the aim of all is to make sales. To do this, they need to consider the physical layout of their stores, merchandising and display, market perception and advertising and promotion. Sales skills and customer service are key to success and need to be based on "people skills" and merchandise knowledge. A retailer's performance is reflected in sales reports, and store audits assess a store's strengths and weaknesses. To do well in both areas, retailers need to calculate trade, series and cash discounts, as well as markups and mark-downs. In the end, it is two financial statements—the balance sheet and the income statement—that indicate how well a retailer is doing.

Appendix: Tenant Audit

Shopping center _____

Evaluator _____

Store _____

Date _____

(1 = poor; 10 = outstanding)

		1st quarter	2nd Quarter	3rd Quarter	4th Quarter
A.	**Store Appearance**				
A1.	Storefront: Are all materials in good repair (windows, moldings, flooring, wood trim, etc.) and maintained according to center standards?				
A2.	Interior: Are all materials in good repair (carpeting, fixtures, lighting, counters, etc.) and maintained according to center standards?				
A3.	Signage: Are all display signage materials done in a professional manner and easy to read?				
A4.	Overall: Is the store dated looking in terms of architectural design, decor, and finishing touches?				
A5.	Dressing rooms: Are they sufficient in number, appropriately placed and designed, neat and tidy?				

(Continued)

(1 = poor; 10 = outstanding)

	1st quarter	2nd Quarter	3rd Quarter	4th Quarter
B. Inventory				
B1. Timeliness: Is the stock fresh and current? Does it include important items of the season, trends, and styles?				
B2. Levels: Is the inventory adequate to convince the customer that the shop warrants a visit? Are seasonal inventories adequate?				
B3. Condition/age: Is there too much "old" merchandise? Is merchandise soiled, damaged, wrinkled, etc.?				
B4. Clearance: Is slow-moving merchandise cleared so current merchandise can be appropriately displayed?				
C. Merchandise Presentation				
C1. Windows: Does the treatment create interest enough to attract shoppers? Do window displays tell a story? Is each display sensitive to color/design? Is display changed regularly?				
C2. Entrance: Is it open, uncluttered, and inviting? Do visible displays invite inspection?				
C3. Check desk: Does the merchandise presentation at check desk offer additional opportunities for sales? Is it neat and organized?				
C4. Stock maintenance: Is it straight, orderly, and appealing to the eye?				
C5. In-store display: Is it well coordinated, featuring appropriate items, and well lit?				
C6. Display tools and their use: Is there proper signing? Are there sufficient fixtures, mannequins, and lighting?				

(Continued)

	(1 = poor; 10 = outstanding)			
	1st quarter	2nd Quarter	3rd Quarter	4th Quarter
C7. Signs: Are advertised items signed, as well as special purchases and promotions? Are the signs properly used?				
D. Sales Staff				
D1. Appearance: Is personnel appearance in keeping with store image, i.e., dress, grooming?				
D2. Salesmanship: Do personnel approach, greet, converse, offer selling facts, counter objections, close?				
D3. Friendliness: Are the salespeople warm, interested in the customers and in their needs?				
D4. Knowledge: Are salespeople trained, knowledgeable about merchandise? Do they use suggestion selling? Do they have a basic knowledge of in-store promotions and advertising?				
D5. Staff levels: Are there adequate salespeople for the hour, day, season?				
E. Management				
E1. Attitude: Is the management working toward the same profit goals as the center and the tenant home office? Do they adhere to center rules? Do they treat customers and staff with respect and consideration? Do they enthusiastically participate in center programs and promotions?				
E2. Experience: Are they qualified to manage size and type of store? Where are their weak/strong areas? Are they making an effort to learn the job better?				

(Continued)

	(1 = poor; 10 = outstanding)			
	1st quarter	2nd Quarter	3rd Quarter	4th Quarter
E3. Turnover: Is there longevity enough to build a trackable management record? If there is high turnover, why? Does the management personality fit with the tenant's retailing philosophy?				
E4. Store policies: Are they clearly displayed and stated where required?				
F. Marketing				
F1. Awareness: Is the management aware of center marketing program and goals? Do they review promotional flyers, calendars, newsletters, etc.?				
F2. Attitude: Does the tenant view the center marketing program as an additional sales aid, attempting to tie in with supplemental advertising programs? Are center programs resented or ineffectively used?				
F3. Participation: Does the tenant take advantage of center promotions, returning questionnaires, attending center meetings, making an effort to appropriately stock and display for mall events?				
F4. Lease: Does the tenant make an effort to meet advertising lease agreements? Is the agreement viewed as a marketing aid or a burden?				
G. Other				
G1.				
G2.				
G3.				

(Continued)

Comments, recommendations, overall evaluation of tenant operations

1st Quarter		2nd Quarter		3rd Quarter		4th Quarter	
Code	Action Taken	Code	Action Taken	Code	Action Taken	Code	Action Taken

Excerpted from *The Library of Shopping Center Marketing Forms.*

Glossary

The glossary that follows is a listing of key definitions compiled from this outline, with several terms not defined in the outline added for your information. The terms are defined within the context of this shopping center management topic.

Alteration costs   Costs incurred in altering and finishing merchandise (usually by a tailor or seamstress) to meet the needs of customers at the time of sale.

Assets   What the business owns. See also "Current assets"; "Fixed assets."

Assortment   The number of different merchandise items within a category. Referred to as the "depth" of merchandise.

Average inventory   An average of the stock on hand at representative dates throughout the year or season.

Balance sheet   Report showing the business's financial position on a specific date.

Cash discounts earned   The discounts for prompt payment of purchases earned on the goods sold during a specified period.

Catalog showroom   A retailer whose showroom is adjacent to its warehouse.

Category specialist (category killer):   A discount store that offers merchandise in a narrow category but a large assortment of merchandise within that category, usually at competitive prices. Dominates a retail category.

Chain   Multiple retail units under common ownership such as department store, specialty store and off-price chains.

Cost   The price at which goods are purchased in the wholesale market or direct from the manufacturer.

Current assets   Assets that can be converted into cash within 12 months.

Current liabilities   Those things owed and due within 12 months.

Direct retailing   Direct mail catalog retailing, TV home shopping, e-commerce business-to-consumer (B2B).

Expenses   Charges involved with running the business. See also "Fixed expenses"; "Variable expenses."

Factory outlet   A retail store operated by a manufacturer usually selling excess inventory that cannot be sold by traditional retailers. Some retailers emulate this concept locating their stores in factory outlet centers to clear away excess inventory of private brands and other merchandise that appeals to "outlet" customers.

Fixed assets   Things used in the business that are not for sale.

Fixed expenses Also called indirect expenses, they are operating expenses that are not affected by increases or decreases in sales volume.

Franchise A contractual agreement that allows the franchisee to operate a retail store using a name and format developed by the franchisor.

Full-line discount store A department store with lower prices on a more limited merchandise assortment and an emphasis on self-service, name-brand merchandise.

Gross Total amount before deductions have been made.

Gross margin The difference between the sales and the total cost of merchandise sold.

Gross profit Markup multiplied by sales price.

Home improvement center A category specialist that combines the traditional hardware store and lumberyard. Provides material and information to do-it-yourselfers to maintain and improve their homes.

Income statement Report showing the business' financial performance over a specific period of time.

Industry averages When the term refers to retail sales, the average national sales figures for a given retail category (broken down by year, month or season).

Initial markup First markup placed on an item (before markdowns).

Inventory   The goods on hand at a specified accounting date. The term may refer either to the physical goods or to their value at retail or cost.

Inventory average   An average of the stock on hand at representative dates throughout the year or season.

Leader   A selected item deliberately sold at a price lower than the one at which the largest total profit on the item could be realized, in order to attract customers.

Leverage   The level of debt against assets.

Liabilities   Those things that can be claimed against the business; what the business owes. See also "Current liabilities"; "Long-term liabilities."

Liquidity   The ability to convert assets into cash.

List price   The manufacturer's suggested retail price.

Long-term liabilities   Those things owed after 12 months.

Loss leader   A selected item that is deliberately sold at less than cost in order to attract customers who will purchase other items at a profit.

Maintained markup   The difference between the net sales and the gross cost of merchandise sold. It is the margin on sales before making adjustments for cash discounts earned and alteration costs.

Markdown   Retail price reduction caused by the inability to sell goods at the original or subsequently determined retail price.

Markup   The difference between the retail selling price of the merchandise and the cost of the merchandise to the retailer.

Mass merchandiser   A value-oriented store that carries merchandise lines in multiple departments, usually with multiple checkout lanes near the store exit and common use of shopping carts.

Merchandise manager   The executive in charge of the merchandise division of a store. In large stores, there are often divisional merchandise managers, each in charge of one of the major merchandise lines.

Merchandise plan   A forecast, usually by months for a six-month season, of the major elements that enter into gross margin. It normally includes the planning of sales, stocks, purchases, markups and markdowns.

Merchandising   The planning involved in marketing the right merchandise, in the right place, at the right time, in the right quantities and at the right price.

Net   What remains after specified deductions from the gross amount.

Net price   Sometimes called retailer's cost price. The amount a retailer must pay for a particular item.

Net profit (or loss)   The amount of money left after all expenses have been paid.

Net worth What the owner actually owns in the business.

Off-price A retailer that offers an inconsistent selection of brand-name, fashion-oriented soft goods at low prices, usually below department store regular price. Off-price retailers typically carry seconds, and items remaining from previous seasons and manufactories' excess inventory.

Operating capital Monies needed to operate the business, as distinct from outlays to finance the business.

Other income Income from sources other than the sale of merchandise.

Overhead Sometimes referred to as fixed expenses beyond cost of sales.

Profit The gain a business realizes over a period, measured in terms of money.

Retail The price at which goods are offered for sale.

Retailer's cost price See "Net price."

Retailing All activities involved in the sale of goods and services directly to the ultimate user for personal, non-business purposes.

Sales The amounts received or accrued to the store in exchange for merchandise sold to customers during an accounting period.

Series discounts A number of discounts offered by the manufacturer to the retailer.

Soft goods   Nondurable goods such as apparel, linens, towels, small fashion accessories. By contrast, hard goods include electronics, appliances and other durable items.

Specialty department store   A department store that has a large selection in more limited categories of merchandise than a traditional department store.

Specialty store   A store that carries a limited number of merchandise categories and provides a high level of service.

Stock turnover   The degree of balance between the retailer's inventory and sales, and the speed with which merchandise moves into and out of a department or store. Average monthly inventory at retail × stock turns = total annual retail sales.

Trade discount   The manufacturer's or supplier's discount from the suggested list price; it is expressed as a percentage.

Traditional department store   A department store that carries home furnishings, men's, women's and children's apparel, home lines and soft goods.

Variable expenses   Also called direct expenses; operating expenses that are affected by increases or decreases in sales volume.

Variety   The number of different merchandise categories within a store or department. Referred to as the "breadth" of merchandise.

Warehouse club   A retailer that provides limited merchandise selection with little service at low prices to individual and business members.